All rights reserved. No part of this book may be reproduced in any form by any means, electronically or mechanical, unless for your personal use without written permission by the author.

All artwork in this coloring book was created by Joy Kelley of HowJoyful LLC.

HowJoyful is a trademark registered in the United States.
For comments or questions, please contact us via email:
hello@howjoyful.com

Published by HowJoyful LLC
ISBN 978-1-7330369-9-3
First Edition: August 2022

NOTE: The author has no oversight over the printing process or paper quality, and while this paper is suited for crayons and color pencils, it's not the best for markers. We have set a dark gray page in the back of each coloring page to help with the color bleeding and see-through of the pages.

www.howjoyful.com/books

how Joyful

Copyright © 2022 by Joy Kelley
HowJoyful® LLC - howjoyful.com

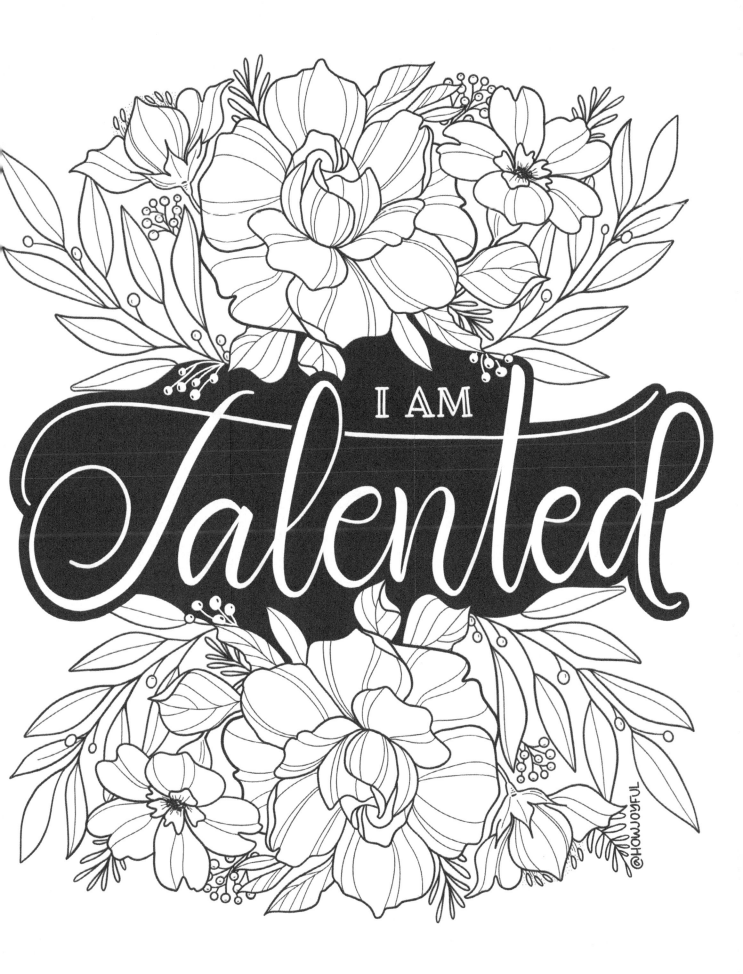

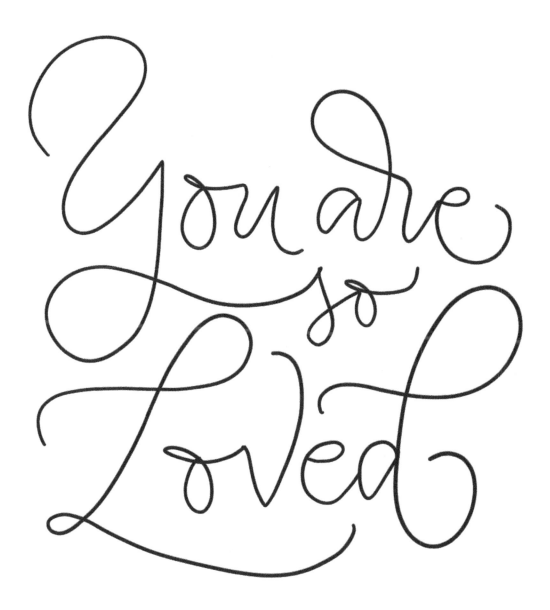

MAY ALL POSITIVE ENERGY
ALWAYS SURROUND EVERY ASPECT OF YOUR LIFE

about the author

Hola! My name is Joy Kelley, I was born in Chile, but I currently reside in the Mountains of Southern California.

I am the mom of 3 little boys and a proud fire wife obsessed with lemon pie. While my degree is in Industrial Design, I have been a full-time lettering artist since 2013.

I have been fortunate to work on fun lettering and calligraphy projects for my shop and design studio (howjoyfulshop.com and howjoyfulstudio.com) and as a freelancer with small and big clients doing branding, editorial, and licensing projects. My work has been featured in publications such as People Magazine, The Today Show, and Project Nursery. I've had my artwork with products for sale nationwide in stores like Nordstrom and TJ-Maxx.

Out of everything I do, teaching lettering, calligraphy, and sharing my love for all things creative is what brings me the most joy and fulfillment. So, If you are interested in those kinds of resources, you can find a lot of free content on my blog (howjoyful.com).

I sincerely hope that you have as much fun coloring each one of these pages as I did drawing each one of the lovely flowers and affirmations =]

Joy Kelley

FIND ME ONLINE
@howjoyful

my books!

Made in the USA
Las Vegas, NV
18 February 2023

67715983R00057